Discard

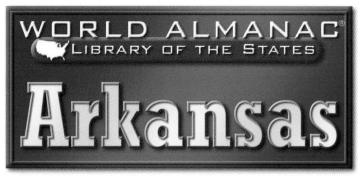

THE NATURAL STATE

by Darice Bailer

Curriculum Consultant: Jean Craven,
Director of Instructional Support,
Albuquerque, NM, Public Schools

WORLD ALMANAC® LIBRARY

Please visit our web site at: **www.worldalmanaclibrary.com**
For a free color catalog describing World Almanac® Library's
list of high-quality books and multimedia programs, call
1-800-848-2928 (USA) or 1-800-387-3178 (Canada).
World Almanac® Library's fax: (414) 332-3567.

Library of Congress Cataloging-in-Publication Data

Bailer, Darice.
　　Arkansas, the Natural State / by Darice Bailer.
　　　　p. cm. — (World Almanac Library of the states)
　　Includes bibliographical references and index.
　　Summary: Presents the history, geography, people, government, economy,
　　social life and customs, and state events and attractions of Arkansas.
　　ISBN 0-8368-5129-3 (lib. bdg.)
　　ISBN 0-8368-5299-0 (softcover)
　　1. Arkansas—Juvenile literature. [1. Arkansas.] I. Title. II. Series.
　　F411.3.B29　2002
　　976.7—dc21　　　　　　　　　　　　　　　　2002069038

This edition first published in 2002 by
World Almanac® Library
330 West Olive Street, Suite 100
Milwaukee, WI 53212 USA

This edition © 2002 by World Almanac® Library.

Design and Editorial: Bill SMITH STUDIO Inc.
Editor: Timothy Paulson
Assistant Editor: Megan Elias
Art Director: Olga Lamm
Photo Research: Sean Livingstone
World Almanac® Library Project Editor: Patricia Lantier
World Almanac® Library Editors: Monica Rausch, Lyman Lyons, Gus Gedatus
World Almanac® Library Production: Tammy Gruenewald, Katherine A. Goedheer

Photo credits: pp. 4-5 Carrick H. Patterson/Hot Springs CVB; p. 6 (left) © PhotoDisc, (top right)
© PhotoDisc, (bottom right) © PhotoDisc; p. 7 (all) © PhotoDisc; p. 9 © Buddy Mays/CORBIS;
p. 10 Library of Congress; p. 11 © PhotoDisc; p. 12 Courtesy of the Library of Congress; p. 13
© ArtToday; p. 14 Little Rock CVB; p. 15 Courtesy of the Library of Congress; p. 17 © Dover;
p. 18 © Steve Liss/TimePix; p. 19 © PhotoDisc; p. 20 (left to right) © Corel, Hot Springs CVB,
© PAINET INC.; p. 21 (left to right) © PAINET INC., Hot Springs CVB, © Corel; p. 23 © PhotoDisc;
p. 26 © PhotoDisc; p. 27 Courtesy of Eastman Kodak; p. 29 Little Rock CVB; p. 31 Courtesy of the
Library of Congress; p. 32 © Michael Rougier/TimePix; p. 33 Little Rock CVB; p. 34 Little Rock
CVB; p. 35 © Doug Hoke/TimePix; p. 36 (top) Hot Springs CVB; p. 36-37 Courtesy of the Library
of Congress; p. 38 © Artville; p. 39 © Underwood and Underwood/TimePix; p. 40 © PhotoDisc;
p. 41 © Reuters/TimePix; p. 42 Courtesy of the Library of Congress; p. 44 (all) © PhotoDisc; p. 45
© PhotoDisc.

Printed in the United States of America

2 3 4 5 6 7 8 9 07 06 05 04 03

Arkansas

The Natural State

Half of Arkansas is still forested, and bears roam the woods the way they did when Spanish explorer Hernando de Soto first visited the area in 1541. He was looking for gold, which he did not find, but there were plenty of unseen riches in the soil.

In the nineteenth century, when settlers began traveling westward across the North American continent, they mainly used northern river routes rather than pass through Arkansas. Few people in the United States knew about Arkansas's hot springs, fertile soil, and mineral resources. Eventually, however, Arkansas's wealth was discovered.

Today, Arkansas has fifty-one state parks, with clear rivers and breathtaking waterfalls. The state has several regional flavors. Fiddles in the highlands in the northwestern corner of the state come alive with Ozark folk music. Farmers still grow cotton along the Mississippi River where plantation owners once made their fortunes before the Civil War. Arkansas's northern neighbor, Missouri, helps give the state a Midwestern flavor.

The capital of Arkansas, Little Rock, lies where the state's northern and southern regions meet, symbolizing Arkansas's position during the Civil War. Arkansans debated whether to join the Union or the Confederacy. In the final year of the war, there were two governments in the state — one Union and one Confederate. The state did not readily free its slaves after the war or give up segregation. African-American liberties were restricted throughout Arkansas until the middle of the twentieth century. Then, in 1957, there was a turning point in the Civil Rights movement in Little Rock, the state capital. That year, federal troops escorted nine African-American students into an all-white high school. Arkansas and the nation moved from segregation to integration. And thirty-six years later, Arkansans celebrated when the state's former governor and native son — Bill Clinton — was sworn in as the forty-second president of the United States.

▶ Map of Arkansas showing the interstate highway system, as well as major cities and waterways.

▼ Bathhouse Row at Hot Springs National Park.

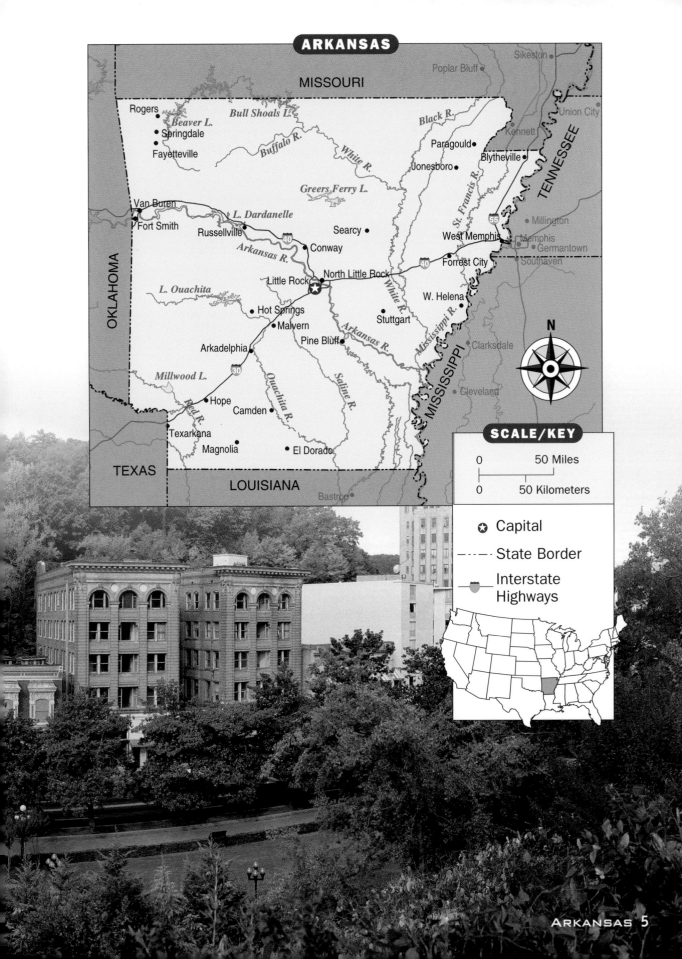

ARKANSAS

MISSOURI

Poplar Bluff
Sikeston
Union City
Kennett
TENNESSEE

Rogers
Beaver L.
Bull Shoals L.
Springdale
Fayetteville
Buffalo R.
Black R.
White R.
Paragould
Jonesboro
Blytheville
Millington

Greers Ferry L.
St. Francis R.
Van Buren
L. Dardanelle
55
Fort Smith
Russellville
40
Searcy
West Memphis
Memphis
Germantown
Conway
Arkansas R.
40
Forrest City
Southaven

OKLAHOMA
Little Rock
North Little Rock
L. Ouachita
White R.
W. Helena
Hot Springs
Malvern
Stuttgart
Arkansas R.
Clarksdale
Arkadelphia
Pine Bluff
30
Saline R.
Cleveland
MISSISSIPPI
Mississippi R.
Millwood L.
Ouachita R.
Red R.
Hope
Camden
Texarkana
Magnolia
El Dorado

TEXAS
Bastrop
LOUISIANA

N

SCALE/KEY

0 ———— 50 Miles

0 ———— 50 Kilometers

⊛ Capital

—··— State Border

▬ Interstate Highways

ARKANSAS 5

Fast Facts

Arkansas (AR), The Natural State

Entered Union

June 15, 1836 (25th state)

Capital	Population
Little Rock	183,133

Total Population (2000)

2,673,400 (33rd most populous state) — *Between 1990 and 2000, population increased 13.7 percent.*

Largest Cities	Population
Little Rock	183,133
Fort Smith	80,268
North Little Rock	60,433
Fayetteville	58,047

Land Area

52,068 square miles (134,856 square kilometers) (27th largest state)

State Motto

"Regnat Populus" — *Latin for "The People Rule"*

State Song

"Arkansas (You Run Deep in Me)," *by Wayland Holyfield, adopted in 1987;* "Oh, Arkansas," *by Terry Rose and Gary Klaff, adopted in 1987*

State Mammal

White-tailed deer

State Bird

Mockingbird

State Insect

Honeybee — *A beehive is one of the symbols on the Arkansas state seal.*

State Tree

Southern pine — *These trees fill Arkansas's forests.*

State Flower

Apple blossom — *Arkansas is one of the nation's most important apple producers.*

State Fruit and Vegetable

South Arkansas vine-ripe pink tomato

State Gem

Diamond

State Mineral

Quartz crystal — *Crystals mined in Arkansas are known as "Arkansas diamonds."*

State Rock

Bauxite — *Arkansas has the largest supply of bauxite in the United States. This rock is used to make aluminum.*

State Musical Instrument

Fiddle — *Arkansas is known for its folk music played on fiddles and banjos.*

State Beverage

Milk

State American Folk Dance

Square dance

State Anthem

"Arkansas," *by Eva Ware Barnett, adopted in 1987*

State Fish

Largemouth bass

PLACES TO VISIT

Texarkana Post Office, *Texarkana*
If you stand in front of the Texarkana post office, you'll actually be standing in two states at once — Texas and Arkansas. That is because the Arkansas state line cuts through the city, and the post office lies in both states.

Clinton Center and Birthplace, *Hope*
Former U.S. president Bill Clinton lived here from the time he was born until he was four years old. The house has been restored to look the way it did when Clinton lived here as a boy.

Central High Museum and Visitor Center, *Little Rock*
Visitors can learn about the historic day in September 1957 when federal troops escorted nine African-American students into this formerly all-white high school.

For other places and events, see p. 44.

For other places and events, see p. 44.

BIGGEST, BEST, AND MOST

- Some of the biggest watermelons in the world grow in Hope, Arkansas. They can weigh more than 250 pounds (113 kilograms).

- Arkansas is the leading rice-grower in the nation and has been for ten years.

- The Sloan burial ground near Paragould is thought to be more than 10,500 years old. It dates back to 8500 B.C.

STATE FIRSTS

- **1832** Hot Springs becomes the country's first national park. It was established forty years before Yellowstone National Park.

- **1972** The Buffalo River becomes the first river in the country to be designated as a national river, thus coming under the protection of the National Park Service.

- **2000** Hillary Rodham Clinton becomes the first First Lady ever elected to the U.S. Senate.

Perfect!

In 1906, an Arkansas farmer discovered diamonds on his property near Murfreesboro. The property is now the Crater of Diamonds State Park. Some diamond experts say that it is the eighth largest diamond-bearing field in the world. Today, visitors to the park can dig for diamonds, and they get to keep what they find. One of the most exciting finds at the park occurred in 1990, when a 3.03-carat diamond was discovered. The stone was purchased by the Arkansas Parks Department and is on display at the park. In 1924, a huge 40.23-carat diamond was found here — the largest in North America. It is the only diamond mine open to the public.

An Embroidered Story

Miss Willie K. Hocker of Pine Bluff designed the Arkansas flag in 1913. The flag was created with a diamond on it because Arkansas was the only state at the time where diamonds were mined. The twenty-five stars on the diamond's border stand for Arkansas's rank as the twenty-fifth state admitted to the Union. The three blue stars below the word *Arkansas* recall that Arkansas was the third state carved out of the Louisiana Purchase. They also symbolize that the Arkansas region has been ruled by three countries: Spain, France, and the United States. The blue star above, added in 1924, signifies that Arkansas was once a Confederate state.

A State Divided

> The wind of the North has twisted and gnarled its branches,
> Yet in the heat of mid summer days, when thunder-clouds ring the horizon,
> A nation of men shall rest beneath its shade...
> And it shall protect them all.
> — "Lincoln," by Arkansas poet John Gould Fletcher, 1919

Historians believe that humans were living in what is now Arkansas around ten thousand years ago. The first peoples in the region were Paleo Indians, who lived during the Ice Age. They hunted animals, such as mammoths, with spears made of a hard stone called novaculite. Around 1000 B.C., Native people who lived along the two rivers now known as the St. Francis and Mississippi Rivers began farming corn, beans, squash, sunflowers, and tobacco. They also built mounds of earth, which were used as bases for temples and sometimes were surrounded by moats or log walls.

Four Native American groups were living in present-day Arkansas when European explorers arrived. The Caddo lived in the southwestern corner of the state, near the Red River. The Osage lived in the Ozark Mountains, and the Tunica were in the southeast. The Quapaw were farmers who lived near the Mississippi River in rectangular houses covered with bark.

Many of the Native Americans living in the region fell victim to diseases that European explorers brought with them to the region. Historians believe that up to 90 percent of the Native Americans who lived in the southeastern United States died of European diseases, such as smallpox and influenza.

The Arrival of Europeans

In 1541, Hernando de Soto, a Spanish explorer, canoed across the Mississippi River into what is now Arkansas, making him the first European to land in the region. He had arrived in present-day Florida in 1539 and was

Native Americans of Arkansas

Caddo
Osage
Quapaw
Tunica

DID YOU KNOW?

How did Arkansas get its name? In 1673, French explorers Jacques Marquette and Louis Jolliet met the Quapaw. The Quapaw called themselves *O-gah-pah*, meaning "downstream people." Marquette and Jolliet's Native American guides, however, called the Quapaw *Akansea* or *Arkansas*. These were Native words meaning "people of the south wind."

exploring the region in search of gold, which he never found. De Soto died of a fever before he could return to Spain.

No other Europeans entered the area until 1673, when two Frenchmen, one a Catholic missionary named Father Jacques Marquette and the other a fur trader named Louis Jolliet, traveled down the Mississippi River. They arrived at the mouth of the Arkansas River hoping to trade with Native peoples and convert them to Catholicism.

Nine years later, in 1682, another French explorer, René-Robert Cavelier, Sieur de La Salle, made his way through the Arkansas region. La Salle was traveling with a group of men, including Frenchman Henri de Tonti. La Salle claimed the entire Mississippi River Valley, including present-day Arkansas, for France. He named the territory Louisiana, after King Louis XIV of France.

Four years later, in 1686, de Tonti returned to the region with a group of soldiers, fur traders, and hunters. At the mouth of the Arkansas River, they established a fur-trading post called the Arkansas Post. The men started trading guns, cloth, and beads with the Native Americans. The post became the first non-Native settlement in the Arkansas region, and de Tonti is now known as the father of Arkansas.

▼ The Caddo built this mound as many as three thousand years ago. The site is now part of Toltec State Park near Little Rock.

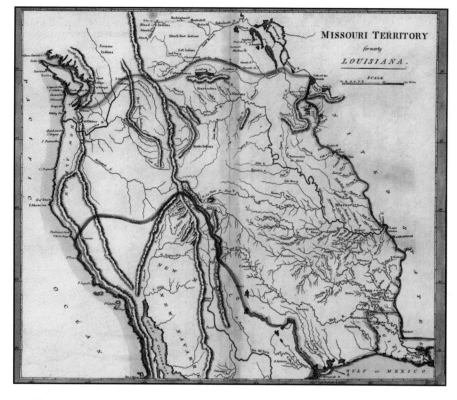

◀ From 1817 to 1819, Arkansas was a part of the Missouri Territory. This map from the period shows what was then known about the area. The red line marks the boundary between American and Spanish possessions.

Despite a French attempt in 1717 to establish a thriving colony, by 1770 fewer than ten European families lived at Arkansas Post.

In 1763, France gave its land west of the Mississippi River — the Louisiana Territory — to Spain and its land east of the Mississippi to England, as part of a treaty that ended the French and Indian War. In 1800, however, France bought back the Louisiana Territory from Spain, only to sell it to the United States three years later. The United States bought all 828,000 square miles (2,144,520 sq km) of the territory between the Mississippi River and the Rocky Mountains for $15 million. The land deal nearly doubled the size of the United States.

In 1812, the northern part of the Louisiana Territory, which included present-day Arkansas, became known as the Missouri Territory. The U.S. government built Fort Smith in present-day Arkansas in 1817, and, in 1819, it carved out Arkansas Territory — a region that included Arkansas and part of what is now Oklahoma and Texas. Arkansas Post was established as the capital of Arkansas Territory, and the first issue of the *Arkansas Gazette* was published there. The *Gazette* was the first newspaper printed west of the Mississippi. Two years later, in 1821,

Big Rock, Arkansas?

Why is the capital of Arkansas named Little Rock? According to an old legend, French explorer Bernard de la Harpe began searching in 1722 for a giant green rock that local Quapaw people had described. La Harpe hoped the rock would turn out to be an emerald. La Harpe did find a large rock on the north bank of the Arkansas River and a small one on the south side, but neither one was an emerald. The two rocks, in fact, served as navigational guides for travelers, marking a shallow spot in the river where it was easy to cross. La Harpe built a trading post near the smaller rock, which he called *petit roche*, or "Little Rock." A settlement grew up around the site, and, in 1821, it became the capital of the Arkansas Territory. The remains of the two rocks can be seen in Little Rock's Riverfront Park.

the territorial capital moved to a more central location, Little Rock.

By 1835, more than fifty thousand settlers were making their homes in Arkansas, enough to give them the right to petition the U.S. government to become a state. Arkansas leaders drew up a state constitution, which was approved by the U.S. government. On June 15, 1836, Arkansas became the twenty-fifth state in the Union. In 1838, the U.S. government forcibly relocated most of the Native Americans in the state west to what was known as Indian Territory. Along with the Quapaw, Osage, and Caddo, other groups who made the painful journey west were those Native Americans who had been relocated earlier to Arkansas from points farther east.

The Civil War

At the time Arkansas joined the Union, American citizens were divided on the issue of whether or not slavery should be allowed anywhere in the nation. Arkansas came into the Union as a slave state, meaning that slavery was legal there. Many Arkansas farmers relied on slave labor to earn a living growing cotton. The state was the sixth-largest producer of cotton. Without slave labor, it would be unprofitable to grow the crop. Cotton farmers, then, tended to side with the Southern states that wanted slavery to be legal. People who lived in the northern highlands, however, were small farmers who did not need slaves. They tended to side with the North and support the end of slavery.

When the antislavery Republican candidate, Abraham Lincoln, was elected president in 1860, Southern states began leaving the Union to form the Confederate States of America. Two of Arkansas's neighbors, Mississippi and Louisiana, joined the Confederacy. In March 1861, the state

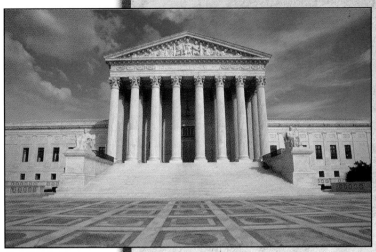

Up from Slavery

Scipio Africanus Jones (1863–1943), the son of a slave woman, rose up from poverty to try a case before the U.S. Supreme Court (*above*). After the Civil War, Jones wanted to go to law school, but the schools he applied to would not admit him because he was African-American. Instead, he studied law informally in attorneys' offices, and he passed the bar examination to become a lawyer. He worked to defend African Americans who could not afford representation. Because of racial prejudice at the time, it was difficult for African Americans accused of crimes to get fair trials, and most could not afford to hire a competent lawyer.

In one of his most famous cases, in 1919, Jones defended twelve African-American men who had been convicted of murders they had not committed. The murders had taken place during a race riot in the town of Elaine. They were found guilty, but Jones appealed their case. The appeal went to the Arkansas Supreme Court and all the way to the U.S. Supreme Court, which ruled that the men had not been given a fair trial and should be set free.

held a special convention to decide whether or not to join the Confederacy. At the convention, the delegates who were pro-Union outnumbered the Confederate delegates, and Arkansas voted against secession. The next month, war broke out between the Union and the Confederacy.

When the Civil War began in April 1861, President Lincoln called for soldiers to enlist in the Union army and fight the Confederates. Although Arkansas had voted to remain in the Union, Arkansans did not want to fight their Southern neighbors. A new convention was held, and this time Arkansas voted to secede.

Not all Arkansans, however, believed in fighting for the Confederacy. About fourteen thousand Arkansans — including five thousand African-Americans — joined the Union army. The state remained divided throughout the war.

At least five major and eleven minor Civil War battles took place in Arkansas. The state was seen as a prize by both sides because of its location on the Mississippi River and because travel to the American Southwest passed through the state. The most important battle occurred in 1862 at Pea Ridge in northwestern Arkansas. The defeat of the Confederate troops in this battle gave the Union a better position from which it controlled Missouri for the next two years.

On September 10, 1863, Union soldiers crossed the Arkansas River and captured Little Rock, forcing the Confederate troops to move their Arkansas state capital to a courthouse in the town of Washington in the southwestern corner of the state. In 1864, during the last year of the Civil War, Arkansas had two state capitals and two governors — one Union and one Confederate.

Reconstruction and the Twentieth Century

When the Civil War ended, Arkansas agreed to outlaw slavery and to guarantee civil rights for all of its citizens, including African Americans. It was officially readmitted as a state in 1868.

▲ The Battle of Pea Ridge took place near the Elkhorn Tavern (*above*). Confederate troops called it the Battle of Elkhorn Tavern. In general, Northern troops named battles after geographic sites, while Southerners named them for human-made landmarks. The site is now a national military park.

Arkansas failed to live up to the spirit of the new civil rights laws, however, and it thwarted efforts by African Americans as well as by poor whites to exercise their rights. The period just after the Civil War, called Reconstruction, was a bitter, unhappy time. Arkansans were still split between those who had sided with the Union and those who had supported the Confederacy. Relations between whites and African Americans were tense and often violent.

Industrialization in the years after the Civil War brought railroads to Arkansas. More than 5,000 miles (8,045 km) of railroads brought workers to the state and made travel easier. The railroads also enabled farmers and factories to send goods to market. Bauxite, which is used to make aluminum, was discovered in 1887 near Little Rock, and mining for this mineral began to play a role in the state's economy. As the twentieth century began, the timber industry also gained importance. In 1904, rice cultivation was introduced, and the state has since become the nation's leading producer of rice. In 1921, the first oil well was drilled in El Dorado, further diversifying the state's economy.

The state's self-improvement projects at this time included the construction of roads as well as water and power lines. A number of colleges were established, including the University of Arkansas at Fayetteville and Henderson College (now Henderson State University) in Arkadelphia. On the political front, in 1917 the Arkansas state legislature gave women the right to vote, own property, and enter into legal contracts.

◄ By the late nineteenth century, Arkansas was using railroads to transport its valuable bauxite to distant markets.

In April 1927, the state experienced a devastating flood. The Mississippi River rose above its banks and spilled over the levees that had been constructed to protect neighboring land from flooding. The flood caused massive damage in several states. In Arkansas, more than 6,000 square miles (15,540 sq km) — 11 percent of the state's land area — were flooded. The flood killed some 90 people and displaced more than 300,000 others in Arkansas.

The Great Depression

Like the rest of the nation, Arkansas suffered during the Great Depression of the 1930s, which began with the stock market crash of 1929. From 1932 to 1938, a drought affected the central part of the United States, including Arkansas, and resulted in crop failures, which made the economic situation even worse.

The New Deal, a group of programs sponsored by the federal government to help ease the effects of the Depression, brought construction and other projects to the state. Artists hired through the New Deal painted murals on the walls of a number of post offices in towns such as Nashville, Van Buren, and Benton. Many families reacted to the hard times by leaving the state in search of better opportunities elsewhere. As they traveled the country, these migrants became known as "Arkies."

◄ Little Rock's Central High School was the setting of one of the most dramatic moments of the Civil Rights movement, as U.S. Army troops enforced desegregation, despite the resistance of Arkansas governor Orval Faubus.

Mobilization for World War II helped to end the Depression. Military training camps opened in the state, and factories worked around the clock to make ammunition and other supplies for the U.S. war effort.

After World War II, when African-American soldiers returned home to Arkansas, they were still forced to use "colored" bathrooms and water fountains, ride in the back on public buses, and attend schools separately from whites. The veterans, along with other African Americans, became increasingly willing to challenge the unfair treatment that made them second-class citizens in the segregated South.

In May 1954, the U.S. Supreme Court declared that separate schools for whites and African Americans were not permitted by the U.S. Constitution. In 1957, a federal court ordered that the all-white Central High School in Little Rock admit African-American students. The governor, Orval E. Faubus, resisted this order, and President Eisenhower sent in the U.S. Army to enforce it. Soldiers escorted nine African-American students into the school. Little Rock became a symbol for the Civil Rights movement, showing that segregation could be defeated. Governor Faubus, however, was reelected in 1964 for a sixth term, still a state record.

Manufacturing had been growing in importance in Arkansas since World War II, and, in the 1960s, earnings from this sector surpassed those from agriculture for the first time. The McClellan-Kerr Arkansas River Navigation System, opened in 1970, eased the transportation of goods through the state.

In 1993, Arkansans watched proudly as Bill Clinton, five-term Democratic governor from Arkansas, was sworn in as president of the United States. He was reelected in 1996.

▲ William Jefferson Clinton (*center*) was sworn in as the forty-second president of the United States on January 20, 1993. His daughter, Chelsea (*left*), and his wife, Hillary (*right*), witnessed the ceremony.

A Rich Heritage

> I believe in Arkansas as a land of
> opportunity and promise.
> I believe in the rich heritage of Arkansas, and
> I honor the men and women who created this heritage.
>
> — *from the Arkansas Creed, a state*
> *pledge of allegiance, 1972*

Between 1990 and 2000, Arkansas experienced a population growth of 13.7 percent, significantly higher than the 3.1 percent population growth across the United States. Many residents from other states move to Arkansas to enjoy the state's mild climate, beautiful scenery, and affordable housing. The population is concentrated in the eastern and central areas and in the northwestern plateau region. The northwestern part of the state is growing the fastest, with people moving in to work at several company headquarters located there, including Wal-Mart and Tyson Foods. According to the U.S. Labor Department, northwestern Arkansas is one of the fastest-growing job markets in the country. Retired people are also attracted to the easy pace of life in Arkansas.

Age Distribution in Arkansas
(2000 Census)

Age	Population
0–4	181,585
5–19	578,924
20–24	181,598
25–44	750,972
45–64	606,302
65 & over	374,019

Across One Hundred Years

Arkansas's three largest foreign-born groups for 1890 and 1990

1890 / 1990

Germany 6,225 — Ireland 2,021 — England 1,569

Germany 2,666 — Mexico 2,507 — United Kingdom 1,971

Total state population: 1,128,179
Total foreign-born: 14,264 (1%)

Total state population: 2,350,725
Total foreign-born: 24,867 (1%)

Patterns of Immigration

The total number of people who immigrated to Arkansas in 1998 was 914. Of that number, the largest immigrant groups were from Mexico (33.4%), India (6.5%), and The People's Republic of China (5.0%).

With much of its land covered by forests, Arkansas is a rural place. A little over half of Arkansas's residents live in cities and towns of more than twenty-five hundred people. Urban areas in the state are concentrated in the northwest, in the southeast, and in the center of the state.

Ethnic Diversity

Arkansas was settled in the nineteenth century mostly by people from other southern states such as Tennessee and Kentucky. This group included people of Irish, Scottish, Welsh, and English heritage. Some of these early settlers were slave owners, and by 1860 about 25 percent of the state's population was African American. In the 1930s, during the Great Depression, many African Americans left the state to find work, and for the next sixty years the African-American population decreased. In recent years, more African Americans have been moving to the state. Some metropolitan areas in the state have populations that are more than 50 percent African American. Since the 1990s, the state's Hispanic population has been increasing dramatically, as Mexicans and Central Americans migrate north in search of work.

▲ The town of Hot Springs got an early start in attracting visitors to Arkansas. Ludovicus Belding began renting rooms in 1832 to people who came to enjoy the area's "healing waters." Some of these visitors became the town's early residents.

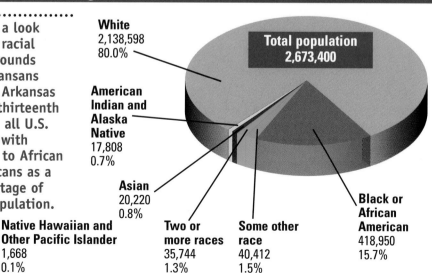

Heritage and Background, Arkansas — Year 2000

► Here's a look at the racial backgrounds of Arkansans today. Arkansas ranks thirteenth among all U.S. states with regard to African Americans as a percentage of the population.

White
2,138,598
80.0%

American Indian and Alaska Native
17,808
0.7%

Asian
20,220
0.8%

Native Hawaiian and Other Pacific Islander
1,668
0.1%

Two or more races
35,744
1.3%

Some other race
40,412
1.5%

Black or African American
418,950
15.7%

Total population
2,673,400

Note: 3.2% (86,866) of the population identify themselves as **Hispanic** or **Latino,** a cultural designation that crosses racial lines. Hispanics and Latinos are counted in this category as well as the racial category of their choice.

Education

During Arkansas's pioneer days, the region did not have many schools. One young missionary, Sophia Sawyer, was determined to teach Cherokee children — especially girls. Around 1840, she founded Fayetteville Female Seminary, and her first students were fourteen Cherokee girls.

Public education was established throughout the state in 1868 as part of Reconstruction. In 1909, Arkansas set up a state board of education to make its educational system better for young people. New public high schools opened up, as well as teacher-training and vocational schools. About one-third of the state budget — 35 percent — is now used for education.

Educational Levels of Arkansas Workers (age 25 and over)	
Less than 9th grade	227,633
9th to 12th grade, no diploma	275,848
High school graduate, including equivalency	489,570
Some college, no degree or associate degree	249,100
Bachelor's degree	132,712
Graduate or professional degree	66,592

▼ Students stroll across the University of Arkansas's Fayetteville campus. Former U.S. president Bill Clinton taught briefly at this school.

Arkansas College, chartered in 1852 in Fayetteville, was the first institution in the state of Arkansas to award college degrees. Arkansas now has ten public universities and several private ones. The University of Arkansas, which opened in 1871, is the largest public university system in the state. The system has six four-year campuses and eight two-year campuses. The university is renowned for its physics and architecture departments and for the medical research that is performed at its medical school in Little Rock. The university is also home to the Razorback sports teams.

Religion

Nearly 90 percent of Arkansans identify themselves as Christians. The first European settlers to arrive in Arkansas were mostly Roman Catholics from France and Spain. After the 1803 Louisiana Purchase, however, new settlers arrived from eastern and southern states, and they tended to be Protestants. Today, more than 40 percent of Arkansans are Baptist. Among other Protestants in the state are Methodists, Episcopalians, and Lutherans. About 0.1 percent of the population are Jewish, and 0.2 percent are Buddhist. While there are few Arkansans who are Muslim, there are several mosques and Islamic centers in the state.

▼ The Arkansas River flows past downtown Little Rock.

From Highlands to Lowlands

> Arkansas, Arkansas, I salute thee,
> From thy shelter no more I'll roam.
> 'Tis a land full of joy and sunshine,
> Rich in pearls and in diamonds rare.
>
> — *"Arkansas," the official state anthem,*
> *written by Eva Ware Barnett, adopted in 1987*

Much of the land in Arkansas is publicly owned and protected. There are fifty-one state parks, three national forests, a national river, two national parks, and eighty-one wildlife management areas. About half of the state, or 18.8 million acres (7.6 million hectares), is covered in forest.

The Mississippi River forms Arkansas's eastern border and separates Arkansas from Tennessee and Mississippi. To the west of Arkansas lie Oklahoma and Texas. Missouri lies to the north, and Louisiana to the south.

Mountains and Valleys

Arkansas is divided into two distinct regions — the highlands, or uplands, of the northwest and the lowlands of the southeast. The highlands are dry and rocky and feature breathtaking vistas, with deep gorges and cascading waterfalls. The Ozark Mountains, in the northwest, are part of a range that extends south from Missouri into northern Arkansas. The mountains, sometimes called the Ozark

Highest Point
Magazine Mountain
2,753 feet (839 m)
above sea level

....
▼ *From left to right:*
a great blue heron in
Arkansas's wetlands;
fireweed and birch
in the mountains
of Arkansas; an old
barn in rural West
Fork; Lake Ouachita,
near Hot Springs
National Park; Lake
Hamilton at sunset;
Arkansas peaches.

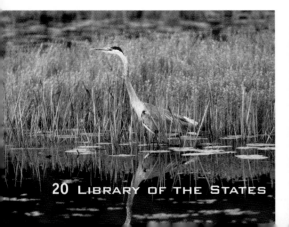

Plateau, are actually a region of high plateaus, with several knob-like summits. The highest points in this range are in the Boston Mountains, which are also the most rugged.

In the nineteenth century, a number of resorts opened in Arkansas's mountains, where visitors could enjoy the hot springs that bubble out of the hills. The most famous of these natural spas is Hot Springs in the Ouachita Mountains, a range directly south of the Ozarks. The warm springs that bubble up in the Ozark and Ouachita Mountains are heated by hot, underground rock.

The Ouachita Mountains are "fold mountains," which form when hard plates beneath Earth's surface are pushed together, crumpling or folding the surface above them.

Arkansas's southeastern lowlands are flat and wet and often flood. The lowlands include parts of the Mississippi Delta and the Coastal Plain. The Coastal Plain was once the coast of the Gulf of Mexico before the coast shifted southward millions of years ago. The delta is mostly flat, with the exception of a 150-mile (241-km) strip of land called Crowley's Ridge, which rises up to 300 feet (91 meters) high.

The fertile Arkansas River Valley lies between the Ozark and Ouachita Mountains. The Arkansas River winds southeast through the valley and empties into the Mississippi River. Starting in the Rocky Mountains in Colorado, the river is the sixth-longest in the country. The McClellan-Kerr Arkansas River Navigation System, completed in 1970, made the river navigable from Oklahoma to Mississippi.

Rivers and Lakes

There are 600,000 acres (242,820 ha) of lakes and 9,700 miles (15,607 km) of rivers and streams in Arkansas. Arkansas has more miles of navigable river than most other states in the country. One of Arkansas's most scenic

---

Average January temperature
Fort Smith: 36°F (2°C)
Little Rock: 40°F (4°C)

Average July temperature
Fort Smith: 81°F (27°C)
Little Rock: 82°F (28°C)

Average yearly rainfall
Fort Smith: 45 inches (114 cm)
Little Rock: 48.5 inches (123 cm)

Average yearly snowfall
Fort Smith: 7.4 inches (19 cm)
Little Rock: 12.2 inches (31 cm)

Major Rivers

Mississippi River
2,340 miles (3,765 km)

Arkansas River
1,459 miles (2,348 km)

White River
720 miles (1,158 km)

DID YOU KNOW?

Water gushes out of Mammoth Spring in northwestern Arkansas at a rate of 150,000 gallons (567,600 liters) a minute, or 9,000,000 gallons (34,056,000 l) an hour!

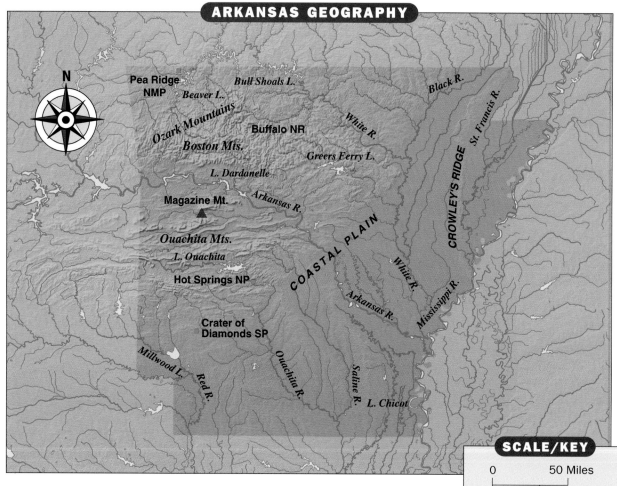

Map labels: Pea Ridge NMP, Beaver L., Bull Shoals L., Black R., St. Francis R., Ozark Mountains, Buffalo NR, White R., Boston Mts., Greers Ferry L., CROWLEY'S RIDGE, L. Dardanelle, Arkansas R., Magazine Mt., Ouachita Mts., L. Ouachita, COASTAL PLAIN, Hot Springs NP, White R., Arkansas R., Mississippi R., Crater of Diamonds SP, Millwood L., Red R., Ouachita R., Saline R., L. Chicot

SCALE/KEY

0	50 Miles
0	50 Kilometers

NMP National Military Park
NP National Park
NR National River
SP State Park
▲ Highest Point
Mountains

rivers is the Buffalo River. This free-flowing stream flows between multicolored 440-foot (134-m) cliffs. In 1972, the U.S. Congress made the Buffalo River a national river, which means that it cannot be dammed. Most of Arkansas's largest lakes are really reservoirs formed by dams. Lake Chicot is the largest natural lake, covering 5,300 acres (2,145 ha). This **U**-shaped lake was once part of a bend in the Mississippi River. About six hundred years ago, however, a high current caused the river to cut across a narrow portion of the bend (or "oxbow"), which separated the remainder of the bend (now Lake Chicot) from the river.

Plants

Arkansas's upland hardwood forests are full of oak, hickory, and sugar maple trees. Cypress, tupelo, and pecan trees grow in the lowlands because their roots can survive constant flooding and swampy conditions. Tulip trees can be found in the northeast on Crowley's Ridge. Shortleaf pine trees abound in the southern part of the state. Arkansas has many beautiful flowering trees, such as magnolias, flowering dogwoods, and dark pink redbuds. Azaleas, bellflowers, yellow jasmine, and other wild flowers add color to the landscape.

Largest Lakes

Lake Ouachita
49,000 acres
(19,830 ha)

Bull Shoals Lake
45,440 acres
(18,389 ha)

Lake Dardanelle
34,000 acres
(13,760 ha)

Animals

The state's ten national wildlife refuges, as well as its many acres of forested land, are home to black bears, foxes, coyotes, and deer. Bobcats, mink, and beavers can be found along the Buffalo National River. Alligators live in Arkansas's swamp lands, while armadillos can be found in the drier areas. Arkansas is also home to 350 types of resident and migratory birds. Great blue herons, turkey vultures, red-tailed hawks, mourning doves, and mockingbirds are some of the birds most often seen. Walleye, bass, and trout attract fishing enthusiasts to Arkansas's lakes and streams. A variety of snakes can be found in the state, including the copperhead, the pygmy rattlesnake, the speckled kingsnake, and the buttermilk racer.

▼ A rushing stream in the Ozarks.

Climate

Arkansas has four distinct seasons but does not experience extreme temperatures in summer or winter. The average yearly temperature ranges from 58° to 65° Fahrenheit (14° to 18° Celsius), making the climate very comfortable. Although summers are humid, the temperature usually stays near 80°F (27°C). In January, the temperature is often above the freezing mark, ranging from 40° to 45°F (4° to 7°C). Despite the mild temperatures, Arkansas does experience extreme weather in the form of tornadoes and thunderstorms, especially in the Arkansas and Mississippi River Valleys.

Land of Opportunity

> There the rice fields are full,
> And the cotton, corn, and hay,
> There the fruits of the field
> Bloom in winter months and May
> — *from "Arkansas," Arkansas's state anthem*

Arkansas has been called the "land of opportunity." The name fits, because Arkansas is laden with precious resources that help create jobs. There are precious mineral mines as well as forests from which lumber can be harvested. In 1887, bauxite was discovered near Little Rock. In 1901, natural gas was found near Fort Smith along the Oklahoma border. Twenty years later, oil was discovered in El Dorado, in the southern part of the state.

Arkansas is not only rich in minerals, but it is also rich in soil nutrients. The Mississippi River Valley is perfect for growing cotton, rice, and soybeans. Agriculture, forestry, manufacturing, and tourism are the state's biggest industries.

Despite the state's wealth of natural resources, Arkansas businesspeople have experienced difficult times throughout the state's history. In the 1930s, during a worldwide depression, banks failed, shops closed, and people lost their jobs. The situation improved during World War II, and farming and mining opportunities grew. The number of manufacturing plants in Arkansas more than doubled in the 1940s and 1950s. Today, most Arkansas residents make a living in the service industry. They work in the fields of education, healthcare, real estate, and retail sales. Two chain stores, Wal-Mart and Dillard's, opened their first stores in the state and have their headquarters there.

Transportation

The topography of Arkansas's highland regions made it difficult to build roads and other components of a transportation system. The lowland areas provided

Top Employers
(of workers age sixteen and over)

Services	29.0%
Manufacturing	22.5%
Wholesale and retail trade	21.3%
Transportation, communications, and other public utilities	7.3%
Construction	6.1%
Agriculture, forestry, and fisheries	4.9%
Finance, insurance, and real estate	4.7%
Public Administration	4.0%
Mining	0.4%

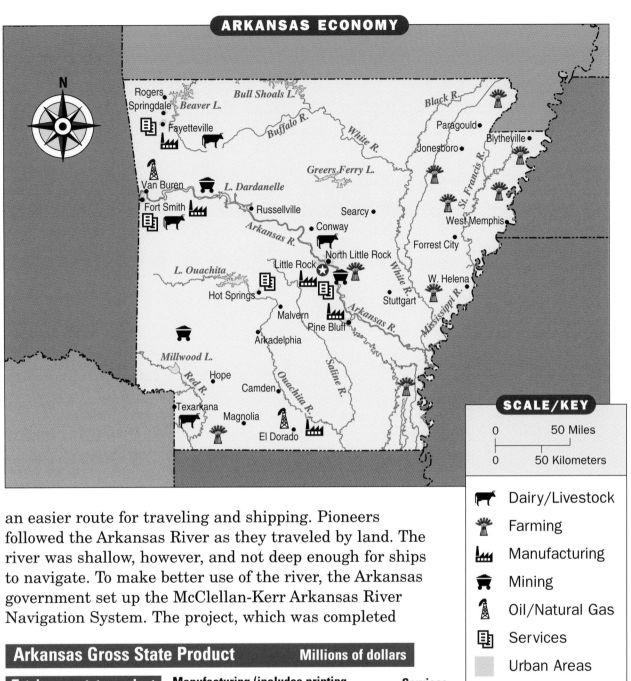

an easier route for traveling and shipping. Pioneers followed the Arkansas River as they traveled by land. The river was shallow, however, and not deep enough for ships to navigate. To make better use of the river, the Arkansas government set up the McClellan-Kerr Arkansas River Navigation System. The project, which was completed

SCALE/KEY

0 — 50 Miles

0 — 50 Kilometers

- Dairy/Livestock
- Farming
- Manufacturing
- Mining
- Oil/Natural Gas
- Services
- Urban Areas

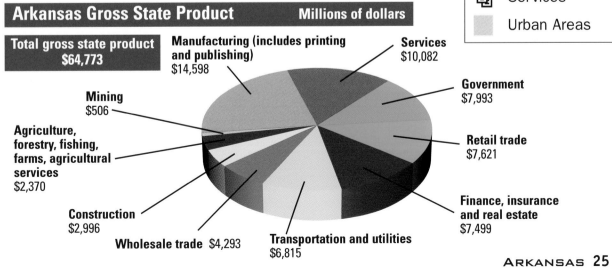

Arkansas Gross State Product — Millions of dollars

Total gross state product $64,773

- Manufacturing (includes printing and publishing) $14,598
- Services $10,082
- Government $7,993
- Mining $506
- Agriculture, forestry, fishing, farms, agricultural services $2,370
- Construction $2,996
- Wholesale trade $4,293
- Transportation and utilities $6,815
- Retail trade $7,621
- Finance, insurance and real estate $7,499

in 1970, deepened the river, enabling ships to travel across the state.

Agriculture

Arkansas is blessed with mild winters and a long growing season. The state has plenty of rainfall, too. Thus, Arkansas is able to grow just about every crop. The state leads the nation in producing rice, providing the nation with a third of its supply. Soybeans are another major crop.

Arkansas also leads the nation in producing chicken broilers for sale. The state is second in the sale of catfish, and third in the number of turkeys raised and sold. Arkansas is also one of the biggest growers of cotton and wheat. Other major agricultural crops are tomatoes, grapes, apples, vegetables, and peaches.

Manufacturing

During and after World War II, factories opened throughout the state. Soon, Arkansas grew from an agricultural to an industrial state. By the 1960s, for the first time, more Arkansas residents earned a living from manufacturing than from farming. Today, 21 percent of the state's work-force makes a living from manufacturing. The state's most profitable products include lumber, paper, furniture, plastics, automobile and airplane parts, electric motors, color television sets, clothing, machinery, and steel.

Natural Resources

The top three natural resources in Arkansas are petroleum, natural gas, and bromine, a dark-red chemical element that is mainly used to make anti-knock gasoline and dyes. Arkansas is the top producer of bromine in the country and supplies half of the world's bromine. Diamonds were discovered in the state in 1906, and Arkansas boasts the only diamond mine in the country that is open to the public. Diamonds are not only valuable for jewelry, but they are also hard enough to be used in drills and cutting tools. For instance, only a diamond is sturdy enough to chisel another diamond into a special shape, such as a heart or square.

Other natural resources found in Arkansas include natural spring water, gravel, and a hard stone called novaculite. The ancestors of today's Native Americans made spears and tools out of this stone. Today, novaculite is used

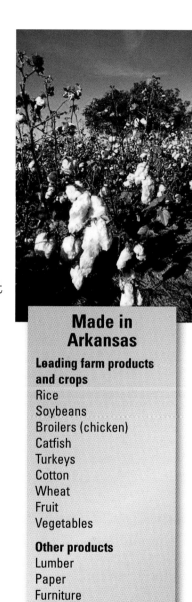

Made in Arkansas

Leading farm products and crops
Rice
Soybeans
Broilers (chicken)
Catfish
Turkeys
Cotton
Wheat
Fruit
Vegetables

Other products
Lumber
Paper
Furniture
Chemicals
Clothing
Plastics
Electronics
Machinery
Steel
Automotive and
  airplane parts

Major Airports		
Airport	Location	Passengers per year (2000)
Little Rock National	Little Rock	2,600,000
Northwest Arkansas Regional	Bentonville	725,175
Fort Smith Regional	Fort Smith	208,062

as a sharpening stone for metal implements. Arkansas also is the only state in the country that mines bauxite.

Tourism

Tourists flock to Arkansas because of its beautiful recreational spots. No wonder, then, that tourism in 2001 brought in close to $4 billion and the state had almost 21 million visitors. Arkansas has 2.6 million acres (1.05 million ha) of national forest. There are also 9,700 miles (15,607 km) of freshwater rivers and streams for fishing, canoeing, kayaking, power boating, waterskiing, and swimming. Vacationers can also raft the state's white-water rivers, such as the Buffalo National River. The Ozark Mountains are the most popular tourist attraction in the state.

▼ The Eastman Chemical Company operations near Batesville employ about seven hundred people in the manufacturing of a wide range of chemical products and by-products.

Land of Promise

> I ask you to join in a re-United States. We need to empower our people so they can take more responsibility for their own lives in a world that is ever smaller, where everyone counts. . .We need a new spirit of community, a sense that we are all in this together.
>
> — *President Bill Clinton, November 4, 1992*

Since its 1836 statehood, Arkansas has had five state constitutions. The first one was written in 1836, when the state was admitted to the Union. The second one was created in 1861, when Arkansas left the Union and joined the Confederacy. Three years later, Union soldiers took over the state government and wrote a new constitution. In 1868, during the Reconstruction period that followed the Civil War, the Arkansas state government gave African Americans the right to vote in a fourth constitution. That constitution was rewritten in 1874 to create a fifth constitution, which still guides the Arkansas state government today.

All five of Arkansas's constitutions have placed the power of the state government in three separate branches — executive, legislative, and judicial.

The Executive Branch

The governor is the head of the executive branch in the Arkansas state government. The lieutenant governor is second-in-command; he becomes governor if anything should prevent the governor from finishing his or her term.

The governor has the power to appoint the adjutant general, the controller, and heads and members of different departments and commissions. The governor is also commander-in-chief of the state's national guard and may call out the national guard in case of an emergency. Responsibilities of the governor's office include reviewing bills presented by the General Assembly and overseeing the state

State Constitution

We, the people of the State of Arkansas, grateful to Almighty God for the privilege of choosing our own form of government, for our civil and religious liberty, and desiring to perpetuate its blessings and secure the same to our selves and posterity, do ordain and establish this Constitution.

— *the Preamble to the Arkansas Constitution, 1874*

budget. After reading a bill, the governor may sign it into law. If the governor vetoes a bill, it does not become law unless a two-thirds majority vote of the General Assembly overrides the veto. A bill also becomes law if the governor fails to act on it within five days.

Other members of the executive branch include the attorney general, who represents the state in legal matters, and the secretary of state, who is the official recordkeeper of the state. The treasurer's and auditor's offices are also part of the executive branch. The treasurer manages the state's revenue, while the auditor monitors all expenses of the state government and pays all of the state's expenses. In Arkansas, the commissioner of state lands is also an office in the executive branch. The land commissioner is in charge of protecting historical landmarks and natural resources, as well as selling property that has been confiscated from owners unable to pay their mortgages.

▲ The Arkansas state capitol is modeled after our nation's capitol. Built in 1911, it stands almost in the exact center of the state. Although the Arkansas capitol is not as large as the U.S. Capitol, it is so similar that moviemakers sometimes use it when they are filming scenes about the U.S. government.

The Legislative Branch

The legislative branch of government in Arkansas is called the General Assembly. It consists of the senate and the house of representatives and is responsible for proposing and passing legislation. There are thirty-five senators elected to the senate, and one hundred representatives serving in the house of representatives. Senators are elected

Elected Posts in the Executive Branch		
Office	Length of Term	Term Limits
Governor	4 years	2 consecutive terms
Lieutenant Governor	4 years	2 consecutive terms
Secretary of State	4 years	2 consecutive terms
Treasurer	4 years	2 consecutive terms
Auditor	4 years	2 consecutive terms
Attorney General	4 years	2 consecutive terms
Commissioner of State Lands	4 years	2 consecutive terms

for four years, and state representatives are elected for two. Senators may not serve more than two terms, and representatives can serve no more than three terms.

Members of the house and senate propose bills, which are then discussed in committees and voted on by first the house and then the senate. The General Assembly considers more than two thousand pieces of legislation in a typical year. Bills address issues such as funding for public education, road construction, and the designation of state parks.

The General Assembly begins its meetings on the second Monday in January every other year. Its legislative sessions cannot go beyond sixty days, unless the General Assembly votes to meet longer and two-thirds of the members of each house approve the decision. Because the assembly does not meet throughout the year, legislators have other jobs. As of 2002, members of the assembly had careers in law, education, the cattle industry, equipment sales, banking, pharmaceuticals, and construction.

The Judicial Branch

The officers of the judicial branch are responsible for enforcing the laws in the Arkansas state constitution. The state is divided into twenty-four circuit court districts and twenty-four chancery court districts. Circuit courts, or courts of law, hear criminal and civil cases that involve damages. Criminal cases are those in which a law has been broken, while civil cases involve disagreements between individuals. Chancery courts, or courts of equity, hear cases that do not involve awards of money.

Arkansas also has courts of appeals, where residents can go if they are unhappy with a lower court's decision. The Arkansas Supreme Court is the highest court and the last court of appeals within the state. One chief justice and six associate justices preside over the supreme court. Supreme court justices and appeals court judges are elected to eight-year terms, while circuit court judges serve six-year terms and chancery court judges serve for four years.

General Assembly			
House	Number of Members	Length of Term	Term Limits
Senate	35 senators	4 years	2 terms
House of Representatives	100 representatives	2 years	3 terms

WILLIAM JEFFERSON CLINTON (1993–2001)
William Jefferson Blythe IV was born in Hope on August 19, 1946, but he grew up in Hot Springs. His father died in an automobile accident three months before he was born. When his mother remarried, Blythe took the last name of his stepfather, Roger Clinton. Clinton was an excellent student and a talented saxophone player. He represented his state on a Boys' Nation trip to Washington, D.C., where he met President John F. Kennedy and began dreaming of a political career.

Clinton graduated from Georgetown University in 1968 with a degree in international affairs and won a Rhodes Scholarship to England's Oxford University. After Oxford, Clinton attended Yale University Law School, where he met his future wife, Hillary Rodham. After receiving his law degree in 1973, Clinton returned to Arkansas and began his political career. In 1976, he was elected attorney general of Arkansas.

At thirty-two, he was the second youngest attorney general in Arkansas history. Clinton served for two years, and in 1978 he was elected governor. He was governor of Arkansas for twelve years. Although Clinton lost his first bid for reelection in 1980 (Arkansas governors served two-year terms until 1996), he won the office back in 1982 and remained the governor of Arkansas until 1992.

That year, Clinton was elected the forty-second president of the United States. When Clinton entered the White House, the U.S. economy began experiencing its lowest inflation rate in thirty years and a period of low unemployment. Major issues in Clinton's administration were the (failed) attempt to introduce national health care, the North American Free Trade Agreement (NAFTA) with Mexico and Canada, and civil wars in Somalia and the Balkans. When he lied about a personal relationship, Clinton became the second president in U.S. history to be impeached by the House of Representatives. Clinton was tried in the Senate, but he was found not guilty.

Local Government

Arkansas is divided into seventy-five counties. The executive officer of each county is a county court judge, who is elected for a four-year term. There are 481 cities and towns in Arkansas. Cities and towns are governed by different systems, including a mayor and city council (Jonesboro), a city manager and board of directors (Hot Springs), and a mayor and board of directors (Little Rock).

Mountains, Museums, and Musicians

> It's the spirit of the people and the spirit of the land,
> It's the spirit of tomorrow and today.
> ... It's the spirit of our fathers,
> it's the spirit of our kids,
> It's the spirit of the music that we play.
>
> — *"Oh, Arkansas," one of Arkansas's two state songs,*
> *by Terry Rose and Gary Klaff, 1987*

Arkansas's mountains, lakes, and rivers attract vacationers to the state year after year. From the pine-covered Ozark Mountains to museums on pioneer life, Civil War battles, and the Civil Rights movement, Arkansas has something for everyone.

Famous Authors and Artists

Arkansas's picturesque towns have long drawn artists and craftspeople to the state. Their work — from paintings to quilts to pottery — is exhibited at Arkansas's many fairs.

Architect Edward Durell Stone (1902–1978) grew up in Arkansas. His designs include Radio City Music Hall in New York City, the John F. Kennedy Center for the Performing Arts in Washington, D.C., and the University of Arkansas Fine Arts Center in Fayetteville.

Arkansas's poets, journalists, and authors have made their marks on the national literary scene. John Gould Fletcher (1886–1950), who was born in Little Rock, was awarded a Pulitzer Prize for Poetry in 1939, the first southern poet to receive that honor. Harry Scott Ashmore (1916–1998) won the Pulitzer Prize in 1958 for his editorials in the *Arkansas Gazette* about the Little Rock Central High School desegregation crisis.

The African-American writer, actress, and singer Maya Angelou has been nominated for a Pulitzer Prize, too, for her book *Just Give Me a Cool Drink of Water 'Fore I Diiie*. Angelou also wrote an autobiography

▼ Arkansan Johnny Cash has recorded more than 1,500 songs. When this photo was taken, at the high point of his career in 1969, his records were selling at the rate of 250,000 a month — faster than those of the Beatles.

called *I Know Why the Caged Bird Sings,* which describes what it was like for her and other African Americans to grow up in Arkansas during a period when economic opportunities were limited and racial segregation was the law. After Bill Clinton was elected president, he invited Angelou to read a poem at his inauguration. She wrote "On the Pulse of Morning" for the occasion. Another famous Arkansas author is John Grisham, who was born in Jonesboro. He writes thrillers about the legal profession, many of which are bestsellers.

Performing Arts

Arkansans and visitors alike enjoy a wide variety of musical and theatrical offerings. Little Rock boasts several theater companies, including the Arkansas Repertory Theatre, the Community Theatre of Little Rock, and The Weekend Theater. Little Rock's Children's Theatre uses both professional and community performers to present a variety of plays for young audiences. In the summer, aspiring young actors can hone their skills at the theater's Summer Theater Academy. Fayetteville is home to the North Arkansas Symphony, which presents a full season of classical and pops concerts each year. The South Arkansas Symphony is headquartered in El Dorado. Many of its concerts feature guest artists from around the globe. The Arkansas Symphony performs a number of classical, pops, and chamber music concerts each year in Little Rock.

▼ Visitors can learn about the history of aviation at Little Rock's Aerospace Education Center, which is also home to an IMAX theatre.

Arkansas has produced its share of great musicians, including Scott Joplin (1868–1917), who was born near Texarkana and invented the musical style known as "ragtime." Other musical greats from Arkansas include country singers Johnny Cash and Glen Campbell and opera singer Barbara Hendricks. Hendricks performed at the White House during Bill Clinton's inauguration.

Museums and Historic Sites

At Ozark Folk Center State Park, local artisans demonstrate how pioneers lived and worked in Arkansas in the nineteenth century. Visitors can watch them carve wood as well as make dolls, musical instruments, furniture, and pottery at one of the many buildings inside the park. The park also has a large auditorium, where audiences can hear traditional folk music concerts.

The Arkansas State University Museum in Jonesboro features the history of the northeastern portion of the state. Its exhibits include Native American artifacts from thousands of years ago. The Arkansas Arts Center in Little Rock displays works by a variety of artists — including European masters — in seven galleries. Little Rock is also home to the Aerospace Education Center and its IMAX theater. The history of aviation is the focus of the exhibits.

The Parkin Archaeological State Park along the St. Francis River offers visitors an interpretation of a Native American village that existed on the site from about A.D. 1300 to 1550 and was possibly occupied by the Casqui.

▼ Arkansas's Old State House was built in the popular Greek Revival style of the mid-nineteenth century. Today, the building serves as a museum dedicated to its time as the state capitol.

There are mounds at the park as well as active archaeological sites where visitors can observe archaeologists during the summer and fall.

Old Washington State Park highlights other eras in Arkansas history. The town of Washington started out as a stop for pioneers headed west on the Southwest Trail. It was later the Confederate Capital of Arkansas.

Today, visitors can tour the restored nineteenth-century town, which features a number of historic structures. They include an 1836 courthouse, a blacksmith shop, and a print museum.

The Fort Smith National Historic Site in the Arkansas River Valley offers a glimpse of what it was like to live in the Arkansas Territory on the edge of the frontier in the early 1800s. Fort Smith — a log and stone stockade — was built in 1817 overlooking the Arkansas River. The U.S. War Department had sent a representative, Thomas A. Smith, to keep peace among the Osage who lived there; the Cherokee, who were forced to move there from the east; and non-Native settlers. In 1871, the old fort was turned into a courtroom and jail for the Federal Court for the Western District of Arkansas. Here, from 1875 to 1896, Judge Isaac C. Parker presided over numerous criminal trials, which resulted in seventy-nine hangings. Guests can see the judge's courthouse and walk around the basement jail.

The Old State House Museum in downtown Little Rock was the state's capitol from 1836 to 1911. The governor of the Arkansas Territory arranged for construction to begin in 1833 — three years before Arkansas became a state. The governor knew that the territory would become a state one day, and he wanted to make sure that Arkansas had a beautiful capitol. In 1836, the building was the site of the first meeting of the state legislature and the inauguration of Arkansas's first governor.

At Pea Ridge National Military Park, visitors can walk over fields that were the site of the largest Civil War battle west of the Mississippi. Here, in March 1862, Union soldiers held back Confederate soldiers, who were on their way to invade Missouri. The battlefield has been preserved, and cannons still stand with their guns pointed. The park has a visitor center and museum, where Civil War uniforms and weapons are on display.

Sports

Arkansas doesn't have major league sports teams. The state does, however, have several minor league teams. Arkansas is home to the Arkansas Twisters arena football team, the Arkansas River Blades minor league hockey team, and the

▲ University of Arkansas Razorback Darnell Robinson dunks in a 1994 NCAA Midwest Regional game against Georgetown University.

Arkansas Travelers minor league baseball team. The Travelers is a double-A farm team for the Anaheim Angels.

Arkansans are enthusiastic supporters of the University of Arkansas sports teams, known as the Razorbacks, a name that comes from wild pigs hunted by settlers. The Razorbacks have triumphed at the national level. The University of Arkansas men's basketball team, for instance, won the 1994 NCAA Championship.

Many famous coaches and athletes grew up in Arkansas. The legendary Paul "Bear" Bryant (1913–1983) coached championship football teams at the University of Alabama during his twenty-five years as head coach. National Baseball Hall of Fame pitcher Jay Hanna "Dizzy" Dean (1911–1974) set a record in 1934, when he won thirty games for the St. Louis Cardinals. That year, Dean and his brother Paul took turns pitching for the team in the World Series, which St. Louis won. Another National Baseball Hall of Famer from Arkansas is Brooks Robinson, a former third baseman for the Baltimore Orioles.

Enjoying Nature

Arkansas is called the Natural State for good reason. Outdoor sportspeople flock to Arkansas's many lakes, rivers, and hiking trails. Lake Ouachita, located in the Ouachita National Forest, is one of the cleanest lakes in the nation. It is used not only for swimming, fishing, and boating, but also for scuba diving. The state's largest natural lake, Lake Chicot in southeastern Arkansas, was created when the Mississippi River changed course hundreds of years ago. Today, birdwatchers, boaters, and fishing enthusiasts enjoy this peaceful lake. There are thousands of miles of waterways in Arkansas that are ideal

▲ The grand hotels of Bathhouse Row in Hot Springs were built between the 1880s and the 1920s. The Hot Springs resort accommodated visitors from around the world who came to "The American Spa" for relaxation and treatment.

for canoeing and rafting. The Buffalo National River, protected by the federal government, has high bluffs on both sides, offering boaters spectacular scenery as they motor, float, or paddle along.

Hikers can explore Arkansas above ground using trails in state and national parks, or they can venture underground for a look at one of the state's many caves. Cobb Cave in the Ozark National Forest and Blanchard Springs Caverns near Mountain View are two caves that offer public tours. The Civil War Cave near Bentonville is interesting to both hikers and historians; it was used by the Confederate army for storing supplies and as a water source.

Other underground assets are Arkansas's many natural springs. At Hot Springs National Park in the Ouachita Mountains, visitors can sit in a natural hot spring where the water is about 100°F (38°C). The springs are formed when rainfall absorbed into the earth is heated on warm rock and gushes out many years later through fault lines on the hillside. In the 1800s, people called Hot Springs "The American Spa" because they believed that the waters had healing powers. It remained a popular therapeutic spa until the 1950s, when the discovery of new medicines cured many of the ailments that had brought people there. Until that time, the city's slogan was "We Bathe the World." A street named Bathhouse Row features eight bathhouses that are protected by the National Park Service. The Fordyce bathhouse has been restored to look the way it did when it first opened in 1915, and it now serves as the park's visitor's center.

Eureka Springs was another famous spa resort, with sixty-three springs. The town built several elegant bath-houses and hotels, including the Crescent Hotel, which opened in 1886. Eureka Springs is nicknamed "America's Victorian Village" and has a historical museum.

"If I could rest anywhere, it would be in Arkansaw, where men are of the real half-horse, half-alligator breed such as grows nowhere else on the universal earth."

— *Davy Crockett, frontiersman, 1835, the winter before Arkansas became a state*

DID YOU KNOW?

Eureka Springs's mountainside location gives it an unusual topography. The lowest street runs 1,000 feet (305 m) below the highest, and no town street crosses another at a right angle. St. Elizabeth's Catholic Church in Eureka Springs is the only church in North America where churchgoers enter through the bell tower!

▼ Within months of its founding on July 4, 1879, the population of Eureka Springs soared to ten thousand people.

Amazing Arkansans

Lift up your hearts.
Each new hour holds new chances
For new beginnings.

— *"On the Pulse of Morning," by Arkansas poet Maya Angelou, 1992*

Following are only a few of the thousands of people who were born, died, or spent much of their lives in Arkansas and made extraordinary contributions to the state and the nation.

SCOTT JOPLIN
COMPOSER

BORN: *November 24, 1868, Bowie County, TX*
DIED: *April 1, 1917, New York City, NY*

Scott Joplin was born in Texarkana and grew up on both sides of the Arkansas-Texas border. As a boy, Joplin took piano lessons and dreamed of writing classical music. In 1902, Joplin wrote his first big composition — a "ragtime" ballet. Ragtime was a new type of American music that combined folk tunes with African rhythm and a touch of Creole music from Louisiana. Musicians played it in New Orleans and on Mississippi river boats. In 1907, Joplin wrote a book called *The School of Ragtime*, which explained this new music. Joplin was nicknamed the "King of Ragtime," and one of his most famous compositions is called "The Entertainer." It was used in a 1970s movie called *The Sting*.

HATTIE WYATT CARAWAY
SENATOR

BORN: *February 1, 1878, Bakersville, TN*
DIED: *December 22, 1950, Falls Church, VA*

Hattie Ophelia Wyatt graduated from college in 1896, at a time when women were just beginning to attend U.S. colleges and universities in

significant numbers. She became a teacher and married Thaddeus Horatio Caraway, a Democrat who was elected to the U.S. House of Representatives from Arkansas, and then to the U.S. Senate. When Senator Caraway died unexpectedly in 1931, Hattie Caraway finished his term. In 1932, she campaigned for her husband's senate seat and won. Caraway was the first woman ever elected to the U.S. Senate. Four years later, she became the first woman re-elected. Caraway — a Democrat like her husband — stayed in office for thirteen years, until 1945.

GENERAL DOUGLAS MACARTHUR
SOLDIER
BORN: *January 26, 1888, Little Rock*
DIED: *April 5, 1964, Washington, D.C.*

Douglas MacArthur's father was a captain and later a lieutenant general in the U.S. Army. As a child, MacArthur lived on several army posts. In 1903, he graduated from West Point Military Academy with top honors. He served in France during World War I and in the Philippines after the war, commanding two areas of U.S. troops. MacArthur was made brigadier general in 1918, major general in 1925, and army chief of staff in 1930. He retired in 1937 but was called back to active duty in 1941. In the Philippines, he led actions against the Japanese. In 1942, MacArthur was put in charge of Allied forces in the southwest Pacific and stationed in Australia. After moving up through the southwest Pacific, MacArthur's forces attacked the Philippines. In 1944, he became a five-star general and soon after commanded all of the U.S. Army forces in the Pacific. He was present when the Japanese surrendered to the United States in 1945. During the Korean War (1950–1953), MacArthur was commander of United Nations military forces in South Korea. President Harry Truman removed MacArthur from his post in 1951 because of a disagreement over strategy. After retiring from active service, MacArthur became a business executive.

DAISY BATES
BORN: *About 1912, Hutig*
DIED: *November 4, 1999, Little Rock*

LUCIUS CHRISTOPHER BATES
BORN: *April 27, 1901, Liberty, MS*
DIED: *August 2, 1980, Little Rock*
CIVIL RIGHTS ADVOCATES

Lucius Bates married Daisy Gatson in 1941. When Gatson was an infant, her mother was murdered by white men, and her father left town to spare the family reprisals that would come if he sought prosecution. Gatson was raised by family friends. Lucius Bates was a journalist and insurance salesperson. In 1942, the couple started a newspaper, the *Arkansas State Press*. Articles in the newspaper spoke out against discrimination and injustice. The Bateses published articles about police brutality against African Americans, joblessness, and attempts to keep African Americans from voting. In 1957, they opened their home to the nine

African-American students who were trying to enroll at the all-white Central High School in Little Rock. Because Daisy Bates courageously escorted the nine students past angry mobs, her home quickly became a target for bombing. Daisy Bates once said, "Now is the time to get smart so that some day we may be able to say not that we shall overcome, but that we have overcome." Both Lucius and Daisy Bates remained active in the Civil Rights movement throughout their lives. Daisy Bates later became president of the NAACP in Arkansas.

WILLIAM FULBRIGHT
SENATOR

BORN: *April 9, 1905, Rothville, MO*
DIED: *February 9, 1995, Washington, D.C.*

James William Fulbright was a U.S. Senator who spent his life working for peace throughout the world. He graduated from the University of Arkansas in 1925 and served as president of the university from 1939 to 1941. He then was elected to the House of Representatives. In 1943, he co-sponsored a resolution that laid the groundwork for the foundation of the United Nations. In 1945, Fulbright was elected to the U.S. Senate. There he served for thirty-two years, from 1945 to 1977. Fulbright started the Fulbright fellowship program, an international exchange and scholarship program for students. He served for fifteen years as chairman of the Senate Foreign Relations Committee. In 1966, he became one of the first lawmakers to speak out against the United States's involvement in the Vietnam War.

DIZZY DEAN
BASEBALL PLAYER

BORN: *January 16, 1910, Lucas*
      (some biographies say 1911)
DIED: *June 17, 1974, Reno, NV*

While Jay Hanna Dean was in the U.S. Army, he practiced his pitching by hurling potatoes at garbage cans. An officer called him "dizzy," and the name stuck. The St. Louis Cardinals signed Dean after he got out of the army, and from 1932 to 1937, Dean was a star. In 1934, he won a record thirty games and was named the National League's Most Valuable Player. Dean's brother Paul also pitched for St. Louis. When a sportswriter asked Dean how the Cardinals could beat Detroit in the 1934 World Series, Dean replied, "Easy. I'll win two and Paul'll win two." The Deans did just that. In 1953, Dean was elected to the National Baseball Hall of Fame.

SAM WALTON
BUSINESSMAN

BORN: *March 29, 1918, Kingfisher, OK*
DIED: *April 5, 1992, Little Rock*

Sam Walton started working when he was seven years old, selling magazines. While in college, he delivered newspapers. After serving in World War II, Walton opened a Ben Franklin five-and-dime store in Bentonville Arkansas. In 1962, he opened the first Wal-Mart Discount City, as the store was known, in Rogers. By 1991, there were seventeen hundred of the stores across the country — making Wal-Mart the country's largest retail store chain. Walton brought discount stores to small towns across America. "You can earn far more at the cheaper retail price than you would have by selling the item at the higher price," Walton said. Walton was one of the richest men in the nation when he died.

Maya Angelou
WRITER

BORN: *April 4, 1928, St. Louis, MO*

Marguerite Annie Johnson got her nickname of Maya from an older brother who called her "mine" or "my sister." Angelou grew up in the small town of Stamps. As a young woman, she moved to San Francisco with her mother, where she became a dancer and took the name Maya Angelou. As a professional dancer, she toured Europe and parts of Africa in a production of Porgy and Bess. After working as a journalist in Egypt and in Ghana, Angelou returned to the United States and wrote "Black, Blues, Black," a television series about African-American history that aired in 1966. In 1970, her autobiographical novel *I Know Why the Caged Bird Sings* was published and has since become a classic. Angelou has published many works of fiction, nonfiction, and poetry, and she has acted in several movies. She was invited to write a poem for the presidential inauguration of Arkansan Bill Clinton. She read the poem "On the Pulse of Morning" at the inauguration. Angelou is a distinguished professor at Wake Forest University in North Carolina.

Johnny Cash
MUSICIAN

BORN: *February 26, 1932, Kingsland*

Johnny Cash grew up in rural Arkansas and studied music at an early age. As a teenager, he performed on the local Blytheville radio station, KLCN. After serving in the U.S. Army in Germany during the 1950s, Cash settled in Memphis, Tennessee, to begin his musical career. He was given a record contract in 1955 and, by 1957, was the top recording artist in the country-and-western category. Some of his most popular songs from this era were "I Walk the Line" and "Folsom Prison Blues." Cash became famous for his deep voice and simple but powerful lyrics and instrumentation. In 1963, he recorded "Ring of Fire," written by Merle Kilgore and June Carter, who was a member of country music's famous Carter Family singers. In 1968, he and Carter were married and she helped him overcome drug addiction. Cash is known as "the man in black" because he always wears black to show his solidarity with all of the world's suffering people. He has won seven Grammy Awards and six Country Music Association Awards. Cash was inducted into the Country Music Hall of Fame in 1980. In 1996, he received a Kennedy Center Award from fellow Arkansan, President Bill Clinton.

Arkansas
History At-A-Glance

1541
Hernando de Soto is the first European in what would later become Arkansas.

1673
Father Jacques Marquette and Louis Jolliet of France sail down the Mississippi River to the mouth of the Arkansas River.

1682
René-Robert Cavelier, Sieur de La Salle, claims the Mississippi Valley, including present-day Arkansas, for France.

1686
A Frenchman named Henri de Tonti sets up camp at the mouth of the Arkansas River.

1717
France brings several hundred colonists to Arkansas in a failed attempt to establish a colony.

1763
Spain takes control of the land west of the Mississippi River, including what is now Arkansas.

1803
The United States buys the Louisiana Territory from France, including what is now Arkansas.

1817
The United States sets up Fort Smith to keep peace among Native American groups and non-Native settlers.

1819
The United States carves out the Arkansas Territory from the Missouri Territory.

1832
President Andrew Jackson makes Hot Springs America's first national park.

1836
Arkansas becomes the twenty-fifth state.

1861
Arkansas breaks away from the Union and joins the Confederacy.

1600   **1700**   **1800**

1492
Christopher Columbus comes to New World.

1607
Capt. John Smith and three ships land on Virginia coast and start first English settlement in New World — Jamestown.

1754–63
French and Indian War.

1773
Boston Tea Party.

1776
Declaration of Independence adopted July 4.

1777
Articles of Confederation adopted by Continental Congress.

1787
U.S. Constitution written.

1812–14
War of 1812.

United States
History At-A-Glance

1936
The first duck-calling contest is held. The contest will become the state's oldest festival.

1964
Orval E. Faubus becomes the first Arkansas governor to be elected to a sixth term.

1993
Former Arkansas governor Bill Clinton is sworn in as the forty-second president of the United States.

1927
Mississippi River floods, killing 98 people in Arkansas.

1868
Arkansas is readmitted to the Union.

1906
Diamonds are discovered on an Arkansas farm.

1957
The United States sends out the U.S. Army to enforce integration at Little Rock's Central High School.

1970
McClellan-Kerr Arkansas River Navigation System opens, making the Arkansas River navigable all the way across state.

2000
Arkansan Hillary Rodham Clinton is the first First Lady elected to the Senate, as a senator from New York.

1874
Arkansas adopts a constitution that is still in force today.

1921
The first oil well is drilled at El Dorado.

1932
Hattie Caraway of Arkansas is the first woman elected to the U.S. Senate.

1800	1900	2000

1848
Gold discovered in California draws eighty thousand prospectors in the 1849 Gold Rush.

1869
Transcontinental railroad completed.

1929
Stock market crash ushers in Great Depression.

1950–53
U.S. fights in the Korean War.

2000
George W. Bush wins the closest presidential election in history.

1917–18
U.S. involvement in World War I.

1941–45
U.S. involvement in World War II.

1964–73
U.S. involvement in Vietnam War.

1861–65
Civil War.

2001
A terrorist attack in which four hijacked airliners crash into New York City's World Trade Center, the Pentagon, and farmland in western Pennsylvania leaves thousands dead or injured.

▼ The Arkansas River at Fort Smith, as seen in 1912.

Festivals and Fun for All

Check web site for exact date and directions.

Arkansas Folk Center, Mountain View

The center is dedicated to preserving southern mountain music and culture. Visitors can see pioneer craft demonstrations such as quilt-making and blacksmithing. The center features a merry-go-round pulled by a mule as well as numerous music and craft festivals throughout the year.
www.ozarkfolkcenter.com

Armadillo Festival, Hamburg

Held in May, this festival features armadillo races, an armadillo look-alike contest, and armadillo trivia for kids. There is also an armadillo weigh-in, where contestants can win a prize for the heaviest armadillo. Additional events include a talent show, a children's pageant, rides, and a fun run.
www.arkansassouth.com/city/hamburg_3.htm

Creepy, Crawly, Cold-blooded Creatures, DeGray Lake Resort State Park, Bismarck

Come for the weekend and learn all about reptiles and amphibians. Grab a turtle, hold a slippery snake, or try to kiss a frog. The park also offers hikes and animal shows.
www.degray.com

Equinox Presentation and Guided Sunset Tour, Toltec Mounds State Park

Watch the sunset over Arkansas's highest mound. Learn about the mound builders who lived in Arkansas more than one thousand years ago and about the alignment of the mounds with solar events. This event is held twice a year, on the spring and fall equinoxes.
www.ArkansasStateParks.com

Johnson County Peach Festival, Clarksville

Held in July, this is the oldest outdoor festival in the state and features a parade, dancing, live music, local foods, a frog-jumping contest, a greased-pig race, and the crowning of Queen Elberta, Miss Arkansas Valley.
www.jocopeachfestival.8m.com

King Biscuit Blues Festival, Helena

This festival in mid-October celebrates the distinctive style of delta blues found in eastern Arkansas. There are three days of live performances by blues and gospel artists.
www.kingbiscuitfest.org

Loose Caboose Festival, Paragould

This annual May festival celebrates the town's history as a railroad center. Events include live music, a backyard barbecue festival, an arts-and-crafts show, and a foot race.
www.loosecaboose.net

Main Street Hardy Great Ozark Duck Race and Hillbilly Olympics, Hardy

Come race 2-inch (5-cm) plastic carnival ducks for a quarter-mile (.4-km) duck race on the Spring River. Then try competing in one of the silly "Olympics." There are contests in skillet tossin', hubcap hurlin', high heel runnin', mop throwin', and more. For more information, call 870-856-3571.

Mt. Magazine International Butterfly Festival, Paris

Held in the state's newest park, this June festival celebrates the more than ninety varieties of butterflies that can be found in this mountainous area. The star of the show is the Diana Fritillary butterfly, which is seen more in Arkansas than in any other part of the country. Events include a butterfly costume contest, dancing, nature walks, and a quilt show. www.butterflyfestival.com

National Wild Turkey Calling Contest and Turkey Trot Festival, Yellville

Watch turkeys released from the roof of the local courthouse. Events at this October festival include a parade, a lip-sync competition, and a turkey lunch. www.yellvilleweb.com

Native American Native Wildlife Festival & PowWow, Turpentine Creek Wildlife Refuge and Foundation, Eureka Springs

This annual June festival celebrates the cultures of Arkansas's Native people. Events include dance contests, storytelling, drumming, and an arts-and-crafts show. www.turpentinecreek.org/PowWow.htm

Original Ozark Folk Festival, Eureka

This October festival features mountain music, a parade, a "Barefoot Ball," and contests such as "Tall Tales Mouth Off," "Pertiest Whistl'n," "Hoop Roll'n," "Longest Beard," and "Biggest Bubble." www.eurekasprings.org/events.htm

Pink Tomato Festival, Warren

This annual summer festival focuses on the official state vegetable and includes tomato stacking, packing, and eating contests, as well as a parade and the coronation of Little Miss Pink Tomato. www.warren.dina.org/geninfo/tomato.html

Rodeo of the Ozarks, Springdale

This July Fourth rodeo features a parade as well as traditional rodeo events such as bareback riding, calf roping, steer wrestling, and bull riding. Cowboys and cowgirls from across the country take part. www.springdale.com/visit/attractions/rodeo.html

Territorial Fair, Historic Arkansas Museum, Little Rock

Learn about Arkansan children from the past and present and participate in games and activities at this May fair. www.arkansashistory.com

Toad Suck Daze, Conway

This spring festival near the Toad Suck lock and dam on the Arkansas River includes toad races, music, arts and crafts, and dancing. www.toadsuck.org

World's Championship Duck Calling Contest, Stuttgart

Duck callers from around the world come to Stuttgart every year during Thanksgiving week for the World's Championship Duck Calling Contest. The contest started in 1936 with seventeen duck callers and a $6.60 hunting coat for first prize. The contest is the oldest festival in the state. www.stuttgartarkansas.com

Books

Beals, Melba Patillo. *Warriors Don't Cry: A Searing Memoir of the Battle to Integrate Little Rock's Central High.* New York, NY: Pocket Books, 1994. Learn about the 1957 integration of Little Rock Central High School from the perspective of one of the nine African-American students who made history there.

Darby, Jean. *Douglas MacArthur.* Minneapolis, MN: Lerner Publications Company, 1989. Learn more about the famous American general who was born in Little Rock and who served the United States in World War I, World War II, and the Korean War.

Gaines, Ann. *William J. Clinton: Our Forty-Second President.* Chanhassen, MN: The Child's World, Inc., 2001. Read the biography of a boy who was born in Hope, Arkansas, and grew up to become the only Arkansan ever elected president of the United States.

Gill, John P. *The Crossroads of Arkansas: A One-Hour Arkansas Perspective.* Little Rock, AR: The Butler Center for Arkansas Studies, 2001. A brief study of Arkansas history.

MacAulay, Ellen. *Arkansas (From Sea to Shining Sea).* New York, NY: Children's Press, 2002. Facts about the people, places, and history of Arkansas.

Web Sites

▶ Official Arkansas state web site
www.state.ar.us

▶ Official state capital web site
www.littlerock.com

▶ Arkansas History Commission & State Archives
www.ark-ives.com

▶ The Arkansas Department of Parks and Tourism
www.arkansas.com
www.arkansaskids.com
www.ArkansasStateParks.com